Signed Graph Approach in Adaptive Transmission Power to Enhance the Lifetime of Wireless Sensor Networks

S. Kannadhasan
A. Babu Karuppiah

ELIVA PRESS

ELIVA PRESS

S. Kannadhasan

A. Babu Karuppiah

A Wireless Sensor Network (WSN) comprises a collection of sensor nodes networked for applications like surveillance, battlefield, monitoring of habitat, etc. Nodes in a WSN are usually highly energy-constrained and expected to operate for long periods from limited on-board energy reserves. When a node transmits data to a destination node the data is overheard by the nodes that are in the coverage range of the transmitting node or the forwarding node. Due to this, the individual nodes might waste their energy in sensing data that are not destined to it and as a result the drain in the energy of the node is more resulting in much reduced network life time. As power is a limiting factor in a WSN, the major challenge in deploying a WSN is to enhance the network life time. So, it becomes inevitable to devise an efficient method of conserving the power. In this paper, a novel algorithm, Signed Graph based Adaptive Transmission Power (SGATP) is developed to avoid redundancy in sensing the data thereby enhancing the life time of the network. The concept of adapting the transmission power based on the distance of the next neighbor is proposed while a node communicates with the Cluster Head during Intrusion Detection. The simulation results show that the network life time is greatly improvised by the proposed method.

Published: Eliva Press SRL

Address: MD-2060, bd.Cuza-Voda, 1/4, of. 21 Chişinău, Republica Moldova

Email: info@elivapress.com

Website: www.elivapress.com

ISBN: 978-1-952751-76-9

Contents

CHAPTER 1

INTRODUCTION

Wireless Sensor Networks (WSNs) have been widely considered as one of the most important technologies for the 21st century. Enabled by recent advances in micro electronic mechanical systems (MEMS) and wireless communication technologies, tiny, cheap, and smart sensors are deployed in a physical area and networked through wireless links and the Internet provide unprecedented opportunities for a variety of civilian and military applications, for example, environmental monitoring, battle field surveillance, and industry process control. A wireless sensor network consists of a possibly large number of wireless devices able to take environmental measurements. Typical examples include temperature, light, sound, and humidity. These sensor readings are transmitted over a wireless channel to a running application that makes decisions based on these sensor readings.

Many applications have been proposed for wireless sensor networks, and many of these applications have specific Quality Of Service (QoS) requirements that offer additional challenges to the application designer. Distinguished from traditional wireless communication networks, for example, cellular systems and Mobile Ad Hoc Networks (MANET), WSNs have unique characteristics, for example, denser level of node deployment, higher unreliability of sensor nodes, severe energy, computation, and storage constraints, which present many new challenges in the development and application of WSNs. In the past decade, WSNs have received tremendous attention from both academia and industry all over the world. A large amount of research activities have bee carried out to explore and solve various design and application issues, and significant advances have been made in the development and deployment of WSNs. It is envisioned that in the near future WSNs will be widely used in various civilian and military fields, and revolutionize the way we live, work, and interact with the physical world. A wireless sensor network (WSN) consists of hundreds to thousands of low-power multi-functional sensor nodes, operating in an unattended environment, and having sensing, computation and communication capabilities. The basic components of a node are a sensor unit, an ADC

3

(Analog to Digital Converter), a CPU (Central processing unit), a power unit and a Communication unit (Figure 1.1).

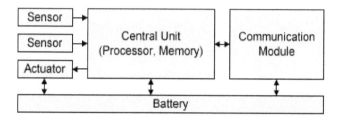

Figure 1.1 Components of wireless sensor networks

Sensor nodes are micro-electro-mechanical systems (MEMS) that produce a measurable response to a change in some physical condition like temperature and pressure. Sensor nodes sense or measure physical data of the area to be monitored. The continual analog signal sensed by the sensors is digitized by an analog-to-digital converter and sent to controllers for further processing. Sensor nodes are of very small size, consume extremely low energy, are operated in high volumetric densities, and can be autonomous and adaptive to the environment. The spatial density of sensor nodes in the field may be as high as 20 nodes/m3.As wireless sensor nodes are typically very small electronic devices, they can only be equipped with a limited power source. Each sensor node has a certain area of coverage for which it can reliably and accurately report the particular quantity that it is observing. Several sources of power consumption in sensors are: (a) signal sampling and conversion of physical signals to electrical ones; (b) signal conditioning, and (c) analog-to-digital conversion.

1.1 Categories of Sensor Nodes:

(i) Passive, Omni Directional Sensors: passive sensor nodes sense the environment without manipulating it by active probing. In this case, the energy is needed only to amplify their analog signals. There is no notion of "direction" in measuring the environment.

(ii) Passive, narrow-beam sensors: these sensors are passive and they are concerned about the direction when sensing the environment.

(iii) Active Sensors: these sensors actively probe the environment.

Since a sensor node has limited sensing and computation capacities, communication performance and power, a large number of sensor devices are distributed over an area of interest for collecting information (temperature, humidity, motion detection, *etc.*). These nodes can communicate with each other for sending or getting information either directly or through other intermediate nodes and thus form a network, so each node in a sensor network acts as a router inside the network. In direct communication routing protocols (single hop), each sensor node communicates directly with a control center called Base Station (BS) and sends gathered information. The base station is fixed and located far away from the sensors. Base station(s) can communicate with the end user either directly or through some existing wired network. The topology of the sensor network changes very frequently. Nodes may not have global identification. Since the distance between the sensor nodes and base station in case of direct communication is large, they consume energy quickly.

In another approach (multi hop), data is routed via intermediate nodes to the base station and thus saves sending node energy. A routing protocol is a protocol that specifies how routers (sensor nodes) communicate with each other, disseminating information that enables them to select routes between any two nodes on the network, the choice of the route being done by routing algorithms. Each router has a priori knowledge only of the networks attached to it directly. A routing protocol shares this information first among immediate neighbors, and then throughout the network. This way, routers gain knowledge of the topology of the network. There are mainly two types of routing process: one is static routing and the other is dynamic routing.

Dynamic routing performs the same function as static routing except it is more robust. Static routing allows routing tables in specific routers to be set up in a static manner so network routes for packets are set. If a router on the route goes down, the destination may become unreachable. Dynamic routing allows routing tables in routers to change as the possible routes change. In case of wireless sensor networks dynamic routing is employed because nodes may frequently change their position and die at any moment.

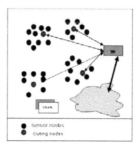

Figure 1.2 : A Wireless Sensor Network structure .

There are four Basic Components in a Sensor Networks:

- An Assembly of distributed or localized sensors
- An Interconnecting network (usually, but not always, wireless based)
- A Central point of Information Clustering
- A set of Computing resources at the central point (or beyond) to handle data correlation, event trending, status querying and data mining.

1.2 Transmitted Power

Wireless sensor networks (WSNs) provide a new class of computer systems and expand human ability to remotely interact with the physical world. Most of the sensors used so far are point sensors which have disc-shaped sensing and communication areas. Energy-efficient communication is discussed in WSNs. Saving energy is very important in WSNs because of the limited power supply of sensors and the inconvenience to recharge their batteries. Methods are proposed to reduce communication energy by minimizing the total sensor transmission power. That is, instead of transmitting using the maximum possible power, sensors can collaboratively determine and adjust their transmission power to reach minimum total transmission power and define the topology of the WSN by the neighbor relation under certain criteria. This is in contrast to the "traditional" network in which each node transmits using its maximum transmission power and the topology is built implicitly without considering the power issue. Choosing the right transmission power critically affects the system performance in several ways. First, it affects network spatial reuse and hence the traffic carrying capacity. Choosing too large a power level results in excessive interference, while choosing too small a power level results in a disconnected network. Second, it impacts on the contention for the medium. Collisions can be mitigated as much as possible by choosing the smallest transmission power subject to maintaining network connectivity. The goal is to find distributed methods to let each sensor decide its transmission power by communicating with other sensors to minimize total sensor transmission power while maintaining the connectivity of the network. It is pointed out that it can maintain the network connectivity, but may not minimize the total sensor transmission power. Then it is enhanced to DTCYC algorithm, where the basic idea is to let each sensor remove the largest edge in every cycle involving it as a vertex. Mathematical proofs show that it can not only maintain the network connectivity but also minimize the total transmission power.

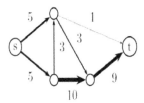

Figure 1.3: Transmitted power in WSN

The source node presented here is indicated as 's'. It has to reach its destination 'T' node by shortest distance calculation and power should be saved. Figure 1.3 shows a sample WSN with arbitrary aspired transmitted power.

Power Efficiency in WSNs is generally accomplished in three ways:

- Low duty cycle operation
- Local/In network processing to reduce data volume (and hence transmission time)
- Multihop networking reduces the requirement for long range transmission since signal path loss is an inverse exponent with range of distance. Each node in the sensor network can act as a repeater, thereby reducing the link range coverage required and in turn the transmission power.

The advantages and disadvantages of WSNs can be summarized as follows:

1.3 Advantages:

- Network setups can be done without fixed infrastructure.

- Ideal for the non reachable places such as across the sea, mountains, rural areas or deep forests.
- Flexible if there is ad hoc situation when additional workstation is required.
- Implementation cost is cheap.

1.4 Disadvantages:

- Less secure because hackers can enter the access point and get all the information.
- Lower speed compared to a wired network.
- More complex to configure than a wired network.
- Easily affected by surroundings (walls, microwave, large distances due to signal attenuation.)

1.5 Applications of Sensor Networks

Military Applications:
- Monitoring minimal forces
- Monitoring friendly force and equipment
- Military theater or battlefield surveillance
- Targeting
- Battle damage assessment

Environmental Applications
- Microclimates
- Forest fire detection
- Flood detection
- Precision agriculture and more..

Health Applications
- Remote Monitoring of physiological data
- Tracking and Monitoring doctors and patients inside a hospital
- Drug administration
- Elderly assistance and more…

Home Applications
- Home Automation
- Instrumented environment

- Automated meter reading and more…

Commercial Applications

- Envirnomental Control in Industrial and office buildings
- Inventory Control
- Vehicle Tracking and detection
- Traffic flow surveillance and more…

1.6   Overview of Sensor technology

Sensor Nodes are almost invariably constrained in energy supply and radio channel transmission bandwidth, these constraints, in conjunction with a typical deployment of large number of sensor nodes, have posed a plethora of challenges to the design and management of WSNs. Some of the key technologies and standards elements that are relevant to sensor networks are as follows:

Sensors

- Intrinsic Functionality
- Signal processing
- Compression, forward error correction, encryption
- Control/actuation
- Clustering and in-network computation
- Self assembly

Wireless Radio Technologies

- Software defined radios
- Transmission range
- Transmission impairments
- Modulation Techniques
- Network Topologies

Standards

- IEEE 802.1.1a/b/g together with ancillary security protocols
- IEEE 802.15.1 PAN/Bluetooth
- IEEE 802.15.3 Ultra wide band (UWB)
- IEEE 802.15.4 ZIGBEE
- IEEE 802.16 WIMAX

- IEEE 1451.5 (Wireless Sensor Working Group)
- Mobile IP

Software Applications

- Operating Systems
- Network Software
- Direct database Connectivity software
- Middleware software
- Data Management Software

1.7   Commercial Generations of Sensor Networks

The Generation of Sensor Networks in 1st ,2nd and 3rd generations are shown in table 1.1. The various Parameters in each generation is clearly indicated.

Table 1.1: Generations of Sensor Networks

Parameters	First Generation	Second Generation	Third Generation
Size	Attach or Larger	Paper back book or smaller	Small, even a dust particle
Weight	Pounds	Ounces	Grams or less
Deployment Mode	Physically installed or air dropped	Hand-placed	Embedded or Sprinkled
Node Architecture	Integrated sensing, Processing and Communication	Integrated Sensing, Processing and Communication	Fully integrated sensing, processing and Communication
Protocols	Proprietary	Proprietary	Standard : Wi-Fi, ZigBee, WiMax, etc..
Topology	Point to Point, Star and Multihop	Client server and peer to peer	Fully peer to peer
Power Supply	Large batteries or line feed	AA batteries	Solar or possibly nanotechnology based
Life Span	Hours, days and longer	Days to weeks	Months to years

CHAPTER 2

ISSUES OF WIRELESS SENSOR NETWORKS

2.1. Hardware and Operating System for WSN

Wireless sensor networks are composed of hundreds of thousands of tiny devices called nodes. A sensor node is often abbreviated as a node. A Sensor is a device which senses the information and passes the same on to a mote. Sensors are used to measure the changes to physical environment like pressure, humidity, sound, vibration and changes to the health of person like blood pressure, stress and heart beat. A Mote consists of processor, memory, battery, A/D converter for connecting to a sensor and a radio transmitter for forming an ad hoc network. A Mote and Sensor together form a Sensor Node. There can be different Sensors for different purposes mounted on a Mote. Motes are also sometimes referred to as Smart Dust. A Sensor Node forms a basic unit of the sensor network

The nodes used in sensor networks are small and have significant energy constraints. The hardware design issues of sensor nodes are quite different from other applications and they are as follow as:

- Radio Range of nodes should be high (1-5 kilometers). Radio range is critical for ensuring network connectivity and data collection in a network as the environment being monitored may not have an installed infrastructure for communication. In many networks the nodes may not establish connection for many days or may go out of range after establishing connection.

- Use of Memory Chips like flash memory is recommended for sensor networks as they are non-volatile, inexpensive and volatile.

- Energy/Power Consumption of the sensing device should be minimized and sensor nodes should be energy efficient since their limited energy resource determines their lifetime. To conserve power the node should shut off the radio power supply when not in use. Battery type is important since it can affect the design of sensor nodes. Battery Protection Circuit to avoid overcharge or discharge problem can be added to the sensor nodes.

- Sensor Networks consists of hundreds of thousands of nodes. It is preferred only if the node is cheap. There are various platforms that are developed considering the above discussed design issues like Mica2, MicaZ, Telos, BT Node and Imotes and MIT µAMPS (µ-Adaptive Multi-domain Power-aware Sensors) . Among them the Berkeley Motes, which is commercially made available by Crossbow Technologies is very much popular and is used by various research organizations.

2.2. Wireless Radio Communication Characteristics

Performance of wireless sensor networks depends on the quality of wireless communication. But wireless communication in sensor networks is known for its unpredictable nature. Main design issues for communication in WSNs are:

- Low power consumption in sensor networks is needed to enable long operating lifetime by facilitating low duty cycle operation and local signal processing.
- Distributed sensing effectively acts against various environmental obstacles and care should be taken that the signal strength, consequently the effective radio range is not reduced by various factors like reflection, scattering and dispersions.
- Multihop networking may be adapted among sensor nodes to reduce the range of communication link.
- Long range communication is typically point to point and requires high transmission power, with the danger of being eavesdropped. So, short range transmission should be considered to minimize the possibility of being eavesdropped.
- Communication systems should include error control subsystems to detect errors and to correct them.

2.3. Medium Access Schemes

Communication is a major source of energy consumption in WSNs and MAC protocols directly control the radio of the nodes in the network. MAC protocols should be designed for regulating energy consumption, which in turn influences the lifetime of the network . The various design issues of the MAC protocols suitable for sensor network environment are:

- The MAC layer provides fine-grained control of the transceiver and allows on and off switching of the radio. The design of the MAC protocol should have this switching mechanism to decide when and how frequently the on and off mechanism should be done. This helps in conserving energy.

- A MAC protocol should avoid collisions from interfering nodes, over emitting, overhearing, control packet overhead and idle listening. When a receiver node receives more than one packet at the same time, these packets are called "collided packets", which need to be sent again thereby increasing energy consumption. When a destination node is not ready to receive messages then it is called overemitting. Overhearing occurs if a node picks up packets that were destined for some other node. Sending and receiving of less useful packets results in control overhead. Idle listening is an important factor as the nodes often hear the channel for possible reception of the data which is not sent.

- Scalability, adaptability and decentralization are other important criteria in designing a MAC protocol. The sensor network should adapt to the changes in the network size, node density and topology. Also some nodes may die overtime, some may join and some nodes may move to different locations. A good MAC protocol should accommodate these changes to the network.

- A MAC protocol should have minimum latency and high throughput when the sensor networks are deployed in critical applications.

- A MAC protocol should include Message Passing. Message passing means dividing a long message into small fragments and transmit them in burst. Thus, a node which has more data gets more time to access the medium.

- There should be uniformity in reporting the events by a MAC protocol. Since the nodes are deployed randomly, nodes from highly dense area may face high contention among themselves when reporting events resulting in high packet loss. Consequently the sink detects fewer events from such areas. Also the nodes which are nearer to the sink transmit more packets at the cost of nodes which are away from the sink.

- The MAC protocols should take care of the well know problem of information asymmetry, which arises if a node is not aware of packet transmissions two hops away.

- MAC Protocols should satisfy the real-time requirements. MAC being the base of the communication stack; timely detection, processing and delivery of the information from the deployed environment is an indispensable requirement in a WSN application. Some popular MAC Protocols are S-MAC (Sensor MAC),B-MAC, ZMAC, Time-MAC and Wise MAC

2.4. Deployment

Deployment means setting up an operational sensor network in a real world environment. Deployment of sensor network is a labor intensive and cumbersome activity as it does not have influence over the quality of wireless communication and also the real world puts strains on sensor nodes by interfering during communications. Sensor nodes can be deployed either by placing one after another in a sensor field or by dropping it from a plane. Various deployment issues which need to be taken care are:

- When sensor nodes are deployed in real world, node death due to energy depletion either caused by normal battery discharge or due to short circuits is a common problem which may lead to wrong sensor readings. Also sink nodes acts as gateways and they store and forward the data collected. Hence, problems affecting sink nodes should be detected to minimize data loss.

- Deployment of sensor networks results in network congestion due to many concurrent transmission attempts made by several sensor nodes. Concurrent transmission attempts occur due to inappropriate design of the MAC layer or by repeated network floods. Another issue is the physical length of a link. Two nodes may be very close to each other but still they may not be able to communicate due to physical interference in the real world while nodes which are far away may communicate with each other.

- Low data yield is another common problem in real world deployment of sensor nodes. Low data yield means a network delivers insufficient amount of information.

- Self Configuration of sensor networks without human intervention is needed due to random deployment of sensor nodes.

2.5 Localization

Sensor localization is a fundamental and crucial issue for network management and operation. In many of the real world scenarios, the sensors are deployed without knowing their positions in advance and also there is no supporting infrastructure available to locate and manage them once they are deployed. Determining the physical location of the sensors after they have been deployed is known as the problem of localization. Location discovery or localization algorithm for a sensor network should satisfy the following requirements :

- The localization algorithm should be distributed since a centralized approach requires high computation selective nodes to estimate the position of nodes in the whole environment. This increases signaling bandwidth and also puts extra load on nodes close to center node.

- Knowledge of the node location can be used to implement energy efficient message routing protocols in sensor networks.

- Localization algorithms should be robust enough to localize the failures and loss of nodes. It should be tolerant to error in physical measurements.

- That the precision of the localization increases with the number of beacons. A beacon is a node which is aware of its location. But the main problem with increased beacons is that they are more expensive than other sensor nodes and once the unknown stationary nodes have been localized using beacon nodes then the beacons become useless.

- Techniques that depend on measuring the ranging information from signal strength and time of arrival require specialized hardware that is typically not available on sensor nodes.

- Localization algorithm should be accurate, scalable and support mobility of nodes.

2.6 Synchronization

Clock synchronization is an important service in sensor networks. Time Synchronization in a sensor network aims to provide a common timescale for local clocks of nodes in the network. A global clock in a sensor system will help process and analyze the data correctly and predict future system behavior. Some applications that require global clock synchronization are environment monitoring, navigation guidance, vehicle tracking etc. A clock synchronization service for a sensor network has to meet challenges that are substantially different from those in infrastructure based networks.

- Energy utilization in some synchronization schemes is more due to energy hungry equipments like GPS (Global Positioning System) receivers or NTP (Network Time Protocol).

- The lifetime or the duration for the nodes which are spread over a large geographical area needs to be taken into account. Sensor nodes have higher degree of failures. Thus the synchronization protocol needs to be more robust to failures and to communication delay.

- Sensor nodes need to coordinate and collaborate to achieve a complex sensing task like data fusion. In data fusion the data collected from different nodes are aggregated into a meaningful result. If the sensor nodes lack synchronization among themselves then the data estimation will be inaccurate.

- Traditional synchronization protocols try to achieve the highest degree of accuracy. The higher the accuracy, then there will be more requirement for resources. Therefore we need to have trade off between synchronization accuracy and resource requirements based on the application.

- Sensor networks span multi hops with higher jitter. So, the algorithm for sensor network clock synchronization needs to achieve multihop synchronization even in the presence of high jitter. Various synchronization protocols which can be found in the literature are Reference Broadcast Synchronization (RBS) and Delay Measurement Time Synchronization protocol.

2.7 Calibration

Calibration is the process of adjusting the raw sensor readings obtained from the sensors into corrected values by comparing it with some standard values. Manual calibration of sensors in a sensor network is a time consuming and difficult task due to failure of sensor nodes and random noise which makes manual calibration of sensors too expensive.

Various Calibration issues in sensor networks are:

- A sensor network consists of large number of sensors typically with no calibration interface.

- Access to individual sensors in the field can be limited.

16

- Reference values might not be readily available.
- Different applications require different calibration.
- Requires calibration in a complex dynamic environment with many observables like aging, decaying, damage etc.
- Other objectives of calibration include accuracy, resiliency against random errors, ability to be applied in various scenarios and to address a variety of error models.

2.8 Network Layer Issues

Various issues at the network layer are :

- Energy efficiency is a very important criterion. Different techniques need to be discovered to eliminate energy inefficiencies that may shorten the lifetime of the network. At the network layer, various methods need to be found out for discovering energy efficient routes and for relaying the data from the sensor nodes to the BS so that the lifetime of a network can be optimized.
- Routing Protocols should incorporate multi-path design technique. Multi-path is referred to those protocols which set up multiple paths so that a path among them can be used when the primary path fails.
- Path repair is desired in routing protocols when ever a path break is detected. Fault tolerance is another desirable property for routing protocols. Routing protocols should be able to find a new path at the network layer even if some nodes fail or blocked due to some environmental interference.
- Sensor networks collect information from the physical environment and are highly data centric. In the network layer in order to maximize energy savings a flexible platform need to be provided for performing routing and data management.
- The data traffic that is generated will have significant redundancy among individual sensor nodes since multiple sensors may generate same data within the vicinity of a phenomenon. The routing protocol should exploit such redundancy to improve energy and bandwidth utilization.
- As the nodes are scattered randomly resulting in an ad hoc routing infrastructure, a routing protocol should have the property of multiple wireless hops.
- Routing Protocols should take care of heterogeneous nature of the nodes i.e. each node will be different in terms of computation, communication and power.

Various type of routing Protocols for WSNs are Sensor Protocols for Information via negotiation (SPIN), Rumor Routing, Direct Diffusion, Low Energy Adaptive Cluster Hierarchy (LEACH), Threshold sensitive Energy Efficient sensor Network protocol (TEEN), Geographic and Energy Aware Routing (GEAR), Sequential Assignment Routing (SAR) and others.

2.9. Transport Layers Issues

End to End reliable communication is provided at Transport layer. The various design issues for Transport layer protocols are :

- In transport layer the messages are fragmented into several segments at the transmitter and reassembled at the receiver. Therefore a transport protocol should ensure orderly transmission of the fragmented segments.
- Limited bandwidth results in congestion which impacts normal data exchange and may also lead to packet loss.
- Bit error rate also results in packet loss and also wastes energy. A transport protocol should be reliable for delivering data to potentially large group of sensors under extreme conditions.
- End to End communication may suffer due to various reasons: The placement of nodes is not predetermined and external obstacles may cause poor communication performance between two nodes. If this type of problem is encountered then end to end communication will suffer. Another problem is failure of nodes due to battery depletion.
- In sensor networks the loss of data, when it flows from source to sink is generally tolerable. But the data that flows from sink to source is sensitive to message loss. A sensor obtains information from the surrounding environment and passes it on to the sink which in turn queries the sensor node for information.

Traditional transport protocols such as UDP and TCP cannot be directly implemented in sensor networks for the following reasons:

- If a sensor node is far away from the sink then the flow and congestion control mechanism cannot be applied for those nodes.
- Successful end to end transmissions of packets are guaranteed in TCP but it's not necessary in an event driven applications of sensor networks.

18

- Overhead in a TCP connection does not work well for an event driven application of sensor networks.
- UDP on the other hand has a reputation of not providing reliable data delivery and has no congestion or flow control mechanisms which are needed for sensor networks. Pump Slowly, Fetch Quickly (PSFQ) proposed is one of the popular transport layer protocol.

2.10 Data Aggregation and Data Dissemination

Data gathering is the main objective of sensor nodes. The frequency of reporting the data and the number of sensors which report the data depends on the particular application. Data gathering involves systematically collecting the sensed data from multiple sensors and transmitting the data to the base station for further processing. But the data generated from sensors is often redundant and also the amount of data generated may be very huge for the base station to process it. Hence a method is needed for combining the sensed data into high quality information and this is accomplished through Data Aggregation. Data Aggregation is defined as the process of aggregating the data from multiple sensors to eliminate redundant transmission and estimating the desired answer about the sensed environment, then providing fused information to the base station.

Some design issues in data aggregation are :

- Sensor networks are inherently unreliable and certain information may be unavailable or expensive to obtain; like the number of nodes present in the network and the number of nodes that are responding and also it is difficult to obtain complete and up-to date information of the neighboring sensor nodes to gather information.

- Making some of the nodes to transmit the data directly to the base station or to have less transmission of data to the base station to reduce energy.

- Eliminate transmission of redundant data using meta- data negotiations as in SPIN protocol.

- Improving clustering techniques for data aggregation to conserve energy of the sensors.

- Improving In-Network aggregation techniques to improve energy efficiency. In-Network aggregation means sending partially aggregated values rather than raw values, thereby reducing power consumption.

19

Data dissemination is a process by which data and the queries for the data are routed in the sensor network. Data dissemination is a two step process. In the first step, if a node is interested in some events, like temperature or humidity, then it broadcasts its interests to its neighbors periodically and then through the whole sensor network. In the second step, the nodes that have the requested data will send the data back to the source node after receiving the request. The main difference between data aggregation and data dissemination is, in data dissemination all the nodes including the base station can request for the data while in data aggregation all the aggregated data is periodically transmitted to the base station. In addition, data aggregation data can be transmitted periodically, while in data dissemination data is always transmitted on demand. Flooding is one important protocol which includes data dissemination approach.

2.11 Database Centric and Querying

Wireless sensor networks have the potential to span and monitor a large geographical area producing massive amount of data. So sensor networks should be able to accept the queries for data and respond with the results.

The data flow in a sensor database is very different from the data flow of the traditional database due to the following design issues and requirements of a sensor network:

- The nodes are volatile since the nodes may get depleted and links between various nodes may go down at any point of time but data collection should be interrupted as little as possible.
- Sensor data is exposed to more errors than in a traditional database due to interference of signals and device noise.
- Sensor networks produce data continuously in real time and on a large scale from the sensed phenomenon resulting in need of updating the data frequently; whereas a traditional database is mostly of static and centralized in nature.
- Limited storage and scarcity of energy are another important constraints that need to be taken care of in a sensor network database but a traditional database usually consists of plenty of resources and disk space is not an issue.
- The low level communication primitives in the sensor networks are designed in terms of named data rather than the node identifiers which are used in the traditional networks.

2.12 Architecture

Architecture can be considered as a set of rules and regulation for implementing some functionality along with a set of interfaces, functional components, protocols and physical hardware. Software architecture is needed to bridge the gap between raw hardware capabilities and a complete system.

The key issues that must be addressed by the sensor architecture are:

- Several operations like continuous monitoring of the channel, encoding of data and transferring of bits to the radio need to be performed in parallel. Also sensor events and data calculations must continue to proceed while communication is in progress.

- A durable and scalable architecture would allow dynamic changes to be made for the topology with minimum update messages being transmitted.

- The system must be flexible to meet the wide range of target application scenarios since the wireless sensor networks to not have a fixed set of communication protocols that they must adhere to.

- The architecture must provide precise control over radio transmission timing. This requirement is driven by the need for ultra-low power communication for data collection application scenarios.

- The architecture must decouple the data path speed and the radio transmission rate because direct coupling between processing speed and communication bit rates can lead to sub-optimal energy performance.

2.13 Programming Models of Sensor Networks

Currently, programmers are too much concerned with low level details like sensing and node to node communication raising a need for programming abstractions. There is considerable research activity for designing programming models for sensor networks due to following issues:

- Since the data collected from the surrounding phenomenon is not for general purpose computing a reactive, event driven programming model is needed.

- Resources in a sensor network are very scarce, where even a typical embedded OS consuming hundreds of KB is considered too much. So programming models should help programmers in writing energy efficient applications.

- Necessity to reduce the run time errors and complexity since the applications in a sensor network need to run for a long duration without human intervention.
- Programming models should help programmers to write bandwidth efficient programs and should be accompanied by runtime mechanisms that achieve bandwidth efficiency whenever possible.

2.14 Middleware

A middleware for WSNs should facilitate development, maintenance, deployment and execution of sensing-based applications. WSN middleware can be considered as a software infrastructure that glues together the network hardware, operating systems, network stacks and applications. Various issues in designing a middleware for wireless sensor networks are:

- Middleware should provide an interface to the various types of hardware and networks supported by primitive operating system abstractions. Middleware should provide new programming paradigm to provide application specific API's rather than dealing with low level specifications.
- Efficient middleware solutions should hide the complexity involved in configuring individual nodes based on their capabilities and hardware architecture.
- Middleware should include mechanisms to provide real time services by dynamically adapting to the changes in the environment and providing consistent data. Middleware should be adaptable to the devices being programmed depending on the hardware capabilities and application needs.
- There should be transparency in the middleware design. Middleware is designed for providing a general framework whereas sensor networks are themselves designed to be application specific. Therefore some tradeoff is needed between generality and specificity.
- Sensor network middleware should support mobility, scalability and dynamic network organization. Middleware design should incorporate real time priorities. Priority of a message should be assigned at runtime by the middleware and should be based on the context.
- Middleware should support quality of service considering many constraints which are unique to sensor networks like energy, data, mobility and aggregation.

- Security has become of paramount importance with sensor networks being deployed in mission critical areas like military, aviation and in medical field.

2.15 Quality of Service

Quality of service is the level of service provided by the sensor networks to its users. Quality of Service (QoS) for sensor networks as the optimum number of sensors sending information towards information-collecting sinks or a base station.

The QoS routing algorithms for wired networks cannot be directly applied to wireless sensor networks due to the following reasons:

- The performance of the most wired routing algorithms relies on the availability of the precise state information while the dynamic nature of sensor networks make availability of precise state information next to impossible.
- Nodes in the sensor network may join, leave and rejoin and links may be broken at any time. Hence maintaining and re-establishing the paths dynamically which is a problem in WSN is not a big issue in wired networks.

Various Quality of Service issues in sensor networks are:

- The QoS in WSN is difficult because the network topology may change constantly and the available state information for routing is inherently imprecise.
- Sensor networks need to be supplied with the required amount of bandwidth so that it is able to achieve a minimal required QoS.
- Traffic is unbalanced in sensor network since the data is aggregated from many nodes to a sink node. QoS mechanisms should be designed for an unbalanced QoS constrained traffic.
- Many a time routing in sensor networks need to sacrifice energy efficiency to meet delivery requirements. Even though multihops reduce the amount of energy consumed for data collection the overhead associated with it may slow down the packet delivery. Also, redundant data makes routing a complex task for data aggregation thus affecting Quality of Service in WSN.
- Buffering in routing is advantageous as it helps to receive many packets before forwarding them. But multihop routing requires buffering of huge amount of data. This limitation in buffer size will increase the delay variation that packets incur while traveling on different routes and even on the same route making it difficult to meet QoS requirements.

- QoS designed for WSN should be able to support scalability. Adding or removing of the nodes should not affect the QoS of the WSN.

2.16 Security

Security in sensor networks is as much an important factor as performance and low energy consumption in many applications. Security in a sensor network is very challenging as WSN is not only being deployed in battlefield applications but also for surveillance, building monitoring, burglar alarms and in critical systems such as airports and hospitals. Since sensor networks are still a developing technology, researchers and developers agree that their efforts should be concentrated in developing and integrating security from the initial phases of sensor applications development; by doing so, they hope to provide a stronger and complete protection against illegal activities and maintain stability of the systems at the same time.

Following are the basic security requirements to which every WSN application should adhere to :

- Confidentiality is needed to ensure sensitive information is well protected and not revealed to unauthorized third parties. Confidentiality is required in sensor networks to protect information traveling between the sensor nodes of the network or between the sensors and the base station; otherwise it may result in eavesdropping on the communication.
- Authentication techniques verify the identity of the participants in a communication. In sensor networks it is essential for each sensor node and the base station to have the ability to verify that the data received was really sent by a trusted sender and not by an adversary that tricked legitimate nodes into accepting false data. A false data can change the way a network could be predicted.
- Lack of integrity may result in inaccurate information. Many sensor applications such as pollution and healthcare monitoring rely on the integrity of the information to function; for e.g., it is unacceptable to have improper information regarding the magnitude of the pollution that has occurred.
- One of the many attacks launched against sensor networks is the message reply attack where an adversary may capture messages exchanged between nodes and reply them later to cause confusion to the network. So sensor network should be

designed for freshness; meaning that the packets are not reused thus preventing potential mix-up.

- In sensor networks secure management is needed at the base station level, since communication in sensor network ends up at the base station.

CHAPTER 3

ATTACKS ON WIRELESS SENSOR NETWORK

3.1 Introduction

Many sensor network routing protocols are quite simple, and for this reason are sometimes even more susceptible to attacks against general ad-hoc routing protocols. Most network layer attacks against sensor networks fall into one of the following categories:

- Spoofed, altered, or replayed routing information
- Selective forwarding
- Sinkhole attacks
- Sybil attacks
- Wormholes
- HELLO flood attacks
- Acknowledgement spoofing

3.2 Spoofed, altered, or replayed routing information

The most direct attack against a routing protocol is to target the routing information exchanged between nodes. By spoofing, altering, or replaying routing information, adversaries may be able to create routing loops, attract or repel network traffic, extend or shorten source routes, generate false error messages, partition the network, increase end-to-end latency, etc.

3.3 Selective forwarding

Multi-hop networks are often based on the assumption that participating nodes will faithfully forward receive messages. In a selective forwarding attack, malicious nodes may refuse to forward certain messages and simply drop them, ensuring that they are not propagated any further. A simple form of this attack is when a malicious node behaves like a black hole and refuses to forward every packet she sees. However, such an attacker runs the risk that neighboring nodes will conclude that she has failed and decides to seek

26

another route. A more subtle form of this attack is when an adversary selectively forwards packets. An adversary interested in suppressing or modifying packets originating from a select few nodes can reliably forward the remaining traffic and limit suspicion of her wrongdoing. Selective forwarding attacks are typically most effective when the attacker is explicitly included on the path of a data flow. However, it is conceivable an adversary overhearing a flow passing through neighboring nodes might be able to emulate selective forwarding by jamming or causing a collision on each forwarded packet of interest.

3.4 Sinkhole attacks

In a sinkhole attack, the adversary's goal is to lure nearly all the traffic from a particular area through a compromised node, creating a metaphorical sinkhole with the adversary at the center. Because nodes on, or near, the path that packets follow have many opportunities to tamper with application data, sinkhole attacks can enable many other attacks (selective forwarding, for example). Sinkhole attacks typically work by making a compromised node look especially attractive to surrounding nodes with respect to the routing algorithm. For instance, an adversary could spoof or replay an advertisement for an extremely high quality route to a base station. Some protocols might actually try to verify the quality of route with end-to-end acknowledgements containing reliability or latency information. In this case, a laptop-class adversary with a powerful transmitter can actually provide a high quality route by transmitting with enough power to reach the base station in a single hop, or by using a wormhole attack. Due to either the real or imagined high quality route through the compromised node, it is likely each neighboring node of the adversary will forward packets destined for a base station through the adversary, and also propagate the attractiveness of the route to its neighbors. Effectively, the adversary creates a large "sphere of influence", attracting all traffic destined for a base station from nodes several (or more) hops away from the compromised node. One motivation for mounting a sinkhole attack is that it makes selective forwarding trivial. By ensuring that all traffic in the targeted area flows through a compromised node, an adversary can selectively suppress or modify packets originating from any node in the area. It should be noted that the reason sensor networks are particularly susceptible to sinkhole attacks is due to their specialized communication pattern. Since all packets share the same ultimate destination (in networks with only one base station), a compromised node needs only to provide a single high quality route to the base station in order to influence a potentially large number of nodes.

3.5 The Sybil attack

An insider cannot be prevented from participating in the network, but she should only be able to do so using the identities of the nodes she has compromised. Using a globally shared key allows an insider to masquerade as any (possibly even nonexistent) node. Identities must be verified. In the traditional setting, this might be done using public key cryptography, but generating and verifying digital signatures is beyond the capabilities of sensor nodes. One solution is to have every node share a unique symmetric key with a trusted base station. Two nodes can then use a Needham-Schroeder like protocol to verify each other's identity and establish a shared key. A pair of neighboring nodes can use the resulting key to implement an authenticated, encrypted link between them. In order to prevent an insider from wandering around a stationary network and establishing shared keys with every node in the network, the base station can reasonably limit the number of neighbors a node is allowed to have and send an error message when a node exceeds it. Thus, when a node is compromised, it is restricted to (meaningfully) communicating only with its verified neighbors. This is not to say that nodes are forbidden from sending messages to base stations or aggregation points multiple hops away, but they are restricted from using any node except their verified neighbors to do so. In addition, an adversary can still use a wormhole to create an artificial link between two nodes to convince them they are neighbors, but the adversary will not be able to eavesdrop on or modify any future communications between them.

3.6 Wormholes

In the wormhole attack, an adversary tunnels messages received in one part of the network over a low latency link and replays them in a different part. The simplest instance of this attack is a single node situated between two other nodes forwarding messages between the two of them. However, wormhole attacks more commonly involve two distant malicious nodes colluding to understate their distance from each other by relaying packets along an out-of-bound channel available only to the attacker. An adversary situated close to a base station may be able to completely disrupt routing by creating a well-placed wormhole. An adversary could convince nodes who would normally be multiple hops from a base station that they are only one or two hops away via the wormhole. This can create a sinkhole: since the adversary on the other side of the wormhole can artificially provide a high-quality route to the base station, potentially all traffic in the surrounding area will be drawn through her if alternate routes are significantly less attractive. This will most likely always be the case when the endpoint of the wormhole is relatively far from a base station. Wormholes can also be used simply to convince two distant nodes that they are neighbors by relaying packets between the two of them. Wormhole attacks would likely be used in combination with selective forwarding or eavesdropping. Detection is potentially difficult when used in conjunction with the Sybil attack.

3.7 HELLO flood attack

A novel attack against sensor networks is the HELLO flood. Many protocols require nodes to broadcast HELLO packets to announce themselves to their neighbors, and a node receiving such a packet may assume that it is within (normal) radio range of the sender. This assumption may be false: a laptop-class attacker broadcasting routing or other information with large enough transmission power could convince every node in the network that the adversary is its neighbor.

For example, an adversary advertising a very high quality route to the base station to very node in the network could cause a large number of nodes to attempt to use this route, but those nodes sufficiently far away from the adversary would be sending packets into oblivion. The network is left in a state of confusion. A node realizing the link to the adversary is false could be left with few options: all its neighbors might be attempting to forward packets to the adversary as well. Protocols which depend on localized information exchange between neighboring nodes for topology maintenance or flow control are also subject to this attack. An adversary does not necessarily need to be able to construct legitimate traffic in order to use the HELLO flood attack. She can simply re-broadcast overhead packets with enough power to be received by every node in the network. HELLO floods can also be thought of as one-way, broadcast wormholes.

Flooding is usually used to denote the epidemic like propagation of a message to every node in the network over a multi-hop topology. In contrast, despite its name, the HELLO flood attack uses a single hop broadcast to transmit a message to a large number of receivers.

3.8 Acknowledgement spoofing

Several sensor network routing algorithms rely on implicit or explicit link layer acknowledgements. Due to the inherent broadcast medium, an adversary can spoof link layer acknowledgments for "overheard" packets addressed to neighboring nodes. Goals include convincing the sender that a weak link is strong or that a dead or disabled node is alive. For example, a routing protocol may select the next hop in a path using link reliability. Artificially reinforcing a weak or dead link is a subtle way of manipulating such a scheme.

CHAPTER 4

GRAPH THEORY

4.1 Definitions and Fundamental Concepts

Graph theory is an extensive and popular branch of Mathematics. It is cross-disciplinary between Mathematics, Computer Science, Electrical and Electronics Engineering and Operations Research which has been applied to many problems in mathematics, computer science, and other scientific and not-so-scientific areas. The basis of graph theory is in combinatory, and the role of "graphics" is only in visualizing things. Graph-theoretic applications and models usually involve connections to the "real world" on the one hand—often expressed in vivid graphical terms—and the definitional and computational methods given by the mathematical combinatory and linear-algebraic machinery on the other.

Graph theoretical concepts are widely used to study and model various applications, in different areas. They include, study of molecules, construction of bonds in chemistry and the study of atoms. It is used in sociology for example to measure actor's prestige or to explore diffusion mechanisms. It is also utilized in biology for monitoring the breeding patterns or tracking the spread of disease, parasites and to study the impact of migration that affect other species, where a vertex represents regions where certain species exist and the edges represent migration path or movement between the regions. Graph theoretical concepts are widely used in Operations Research. For example, in the traveling salesman problem, the shortest spanning tree in a weighted graph obtains an optimal match of jobs and men. It is also used in modeling transport networks, activity networks and theory of games. The network activity is used to solve large number of combinatorial problems. The best well known problems are PERT (Project Evaluation Review Technique) and CPM (Critical Path Method). Computer science applications also use graph theoretical ideas in research areas such as data mining, image segmentation, clustering, image capturing, networking etc., In the same way the most important concept of graph coloring is utilized in resource allocation, scheduling. Also, paths, walks and circuits in graph theory are used in tremendous applications say database design concepts and resource networking.

Graphs and networks are all around us including technological networks like the internet, power grids, telephone networks and transportation networks, social networks like social graphs and affiliation networks, information networks like world wide web, citation graphs and patent networks, biological networks like biochemical networks, neural networks and food webs and many more. Graphs provide a structural model that makes it possible to analyze and understand how many separate systems act together.

4.2 Graph theory and Networks

Conceptually, a graph is formed by vertices and edges connecting the vertices. Formally, a graph is a pair of sets (V, E), where V is the *set of vertices* and E is the *set of edges*, formed by pairs of vertices. E is a *multi-set*, in other words, its elements can occur more than once so that every element has a *multiplicity*. A computer network, or simply a network, is a collection of computers and other hardware components interconnected by communication channels that allow sharing of resources and information. Simply, more than one computer interconnected through a communication medium for information interchange is called a computer network. Using graph the nodes of the network are represented as a collection of points, called vertices, and a collection of lines, called arcs or edges represent the communication link connecting these points.

The major role of graph theory in computer applications is the development of graph algorithms. Numerous algorithms are used to solve problems that are modeled in the form of graphs. These algorithms are used to solve the graph theoretical concepts which intern used to solve the corresponding computer science application problems.

Some algorithms are as follows:

- Shortest path algorithm in a network
- Finding a minimum spanning tree
- Finding graph planarity
- Algorithms to find adjacency matrices.
- Algorithms to find the connectedness
- Algorithms to find the cycles in a graph
- Algorithms for searching an element in a data structure

One of the usages of graph theory is to give a unified formalism for many very different looking problems. This leads to the development of new algorithms and new theorems that can be used in umpteen applications.

Graph theory started with Euler who was asked to find a nice path across the seven Konigsberg Bridges in Figure 4.1.

Figure 4.1: Koningsberg Bridges

The Eulerian path should cross over reach of the seven bridges exactly once in Figure 4.2.

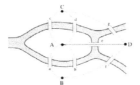

Figure 4.2: Eulerian Path

But now graph theory is used for finding communities in networks in Figure 4.3.

Figure 4.3: Graph Theory in Networks

A graph G = (V,E) is a pair of vertices (or nodes) V and a set of edges E, assumed finite i.e. |V| = n and |E| = m in Figure 4.4.

33

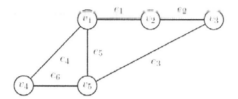

Figure 4.4: Simple Graph Theory in Networks

- Here V(G) = {v1, v2, ..., v5} and E(G) = {e1, e2, ..., e6}.
- An edge $e_k = (v_i, v_j)$ is incident with the vertices v_i and v_j.
- A simple graph has no self-loops or multiple edges like below.

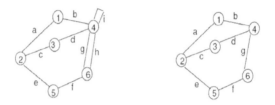

Figure 4.5: Simple Graph Theory with Multiple Edges

4.3 Representation of Graphs

A graph G = (V,E) is often represented by its adjacency matrix. It is an n × n matrix A with A(i, j) = 1 if f (i, j) ∈ E in Figure 4.6.

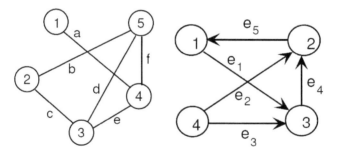

Figure 4.6 Representation of Graph

One can also use a sparse matrix representation of A and T.This is in fact nothing but a list of edges, organized e.g. by nodes.

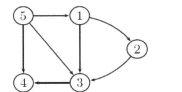

$$V(1) = \{2,3\}$$
$$V(2) = \{3\}$$
$$V(3) = \{4\}$$
$$V(4) = \emptyset$$
$$V(5) = \{1,3,4\}$$

Notice that the size of the representation of a graph is thus linear in the number of edges in the graph (i.e. in m = |E|). To be more precise, one should count the number of bits needed to represent all entries :

$$L = (n + m) \log n$$

Since one needs log n bits to represent the vertex pointers.

4.4 Algorithm Used in Graph Theory

Verify (strong) connectivity of a graph based on its adjacency list in Figure 4.7.

$V(1) = \{2,4,5,6\}$
$V(2) = \{1,5\}$
$V(3) = \{4,7,8\}$
$V(4) = \{1,3,6\}$
$V(5) = \{1,2,6\}$
$V(6) = \{1,4,5\}$
$V(7) = \{3\}$
$V(8) = \{3\}$

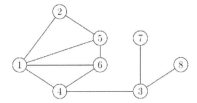

Figure 4.7: Simple Calculation of Networks

Algorithm : 1.GenericSearch(G,s)
mark(s); L := {s}
while L 6= ;
do
choose u 2 L;
if 9(u, v) such that v is unmarked **then**
mark(v); L := L [{v};
else
L := L\{u};
end if

35

end while

4.5 Shortest Path

Find the shortest total length of a path between two nodes of a directed graph with lengths associated with each edge in Figure 4.8.

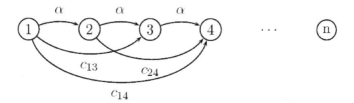

Figure 4.8 Example of Shortest Path Graph

Other example : Find the best production policy for a plant with a monthly demand d_i , a launching cost f_i , a storage cost h_i and a unit price p_i , for each period $i = 1, \dots , n$. In the path below, we are e.g. producing in stages 1, 4 and 5 in Figure 4.9.

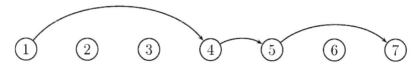

Figure 4.9: Shortest Path Calculation Using Graph

A cost is associated with each section. For the path (1,4) it is e.g. $c14 = f1 + p1(d1 + d2 + d3) + h1(d2 + d3) + h2(d3)$ which is the fixed cost + the production cost in periods 1, 2 and 3 + storage costs at the end of periods 1 and 2. The minimization of the total cost amounts to a shortest path problem in a graph combining paths as above.

4.6 Networks and Flows

A network is a directed graph $N = (V,E)$ with a source node s (with $d_{out}(s) > 0$) and a terminal node t (with $d_{in}(t) > 0$) in Figure 4.10.

Moreover each edge has a strictly positive capacity $c(e) > 0$.

36

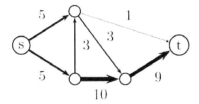

Figure 4.10 : Networks flows in Graph Theory

A flow f : $V^2 = R^+$ is associated with each edge e = (u, v) s.t.

- For each edge e $\in$ E we have $0 \le f(e) \le c(e)$.
- For each intermediate node v $\in$ V\{s, t} the in- and out-flow at that node.

The total flow F of the network is then what leaves s or reaches t,

$$F(N) := \sum f(s, u) - f(u, s) = \sum f(u,t) - f(t,u)$$

4.7 Applications of Graph Theory

- Binary Tree
- Construction of Reliable Communication Networks
- The Lame Duck Airlines Problem
- Assignment of Radio Frequencies
- Fast Register Allocation for Computer Programming
- Scheduling an Oral Examination
- Latin Square
- Timetabling Problem
- Transportation Problem
- Maritime Traffic
- Membership Problem
- Mathematical Analysis

CHAPTER 5

RELATED WORK

Many algorithms and techniques have been developed that utilize power in an efficient manner. Some of the techniques and methods that are used to design the proposed algorithm are discussed here to know how power is dynamically reconciled to meet the constraint of power depletion in nodes of the network.

Sorooshyari et.al. [1] have addressed the problem of adjusting the transmission power level at each wireless radio interface on a per packet basis, based on user and network applications. They have put forth a power control policy that enables a user to address various user – centric and network – centric objectives. The proposed power control policy is optimal with respect to users dynamically allocating transmit power.

Correia et. al. in [2] have devised two transmission power control protocols for WSNs, which can be embedded into any existing MAC protocol. The first, called Hybrid, calculates the ideal transmission power using a closed control loop that iterates over the available transmissions powers in order to maintain a target link quality. The second, called AEWMA, employs calculations to determine the ideal transmission power based on the reception transmission power and average noise.

Arnab Nandi et. al. [3] have propose power based transmission scheme for WSN where transmit power is adapted depending on node density and channel conditions so as to maintain a desired level of signal detection probability at a receiving node as demanded by sensing range. They have compared the energy level performance and the proposed transmit power schemes. With respect to energy consumption, they have shown that the proposed scheme consumes less energy than FTPS in moderate and high node spatial density region.

In [4], [5] the authors have addressed examples of the Dynamic Transmission Power Control DTPC WSN.

In [6] Kayhan Erciyes et. al have utilized the concept of Graph theory and have performed Clustering of sensor nodes using dominating sets of the theory. They have provided the survey on the clustering algorithms using graph theory.

The authors Jin Wang et.al in [7] proposes a novel transmission power control approach named local transmit power assignment (LA-TPA). considers both the path loss exponent and the energy control coefficient in order to characterize the minimum cover of each node more accurately and precisely according to network environment and application scenario of the network. Moreover, it provides a self-healing function that makes network maintain the best performance for a long time when few of the nodes exhaust their energy or a fresh batch of is deployed.

In [8], for dynamically adjusting transmission power level on per node basis, two algorithms LMN and LMA been evaluated and it is shown that the developed algorithms out perform fixed power level assignment.

In [10], the authors have thrown light on the to find an optimal transmission power to control the connectivity properties of the network or a part of it, which could be power per node, per link, or a single power level for the whole network.

Algorithms have been framed in [11] for minimum-energy paths for a reliable packet delivery leading to reliable wireless communication based power, proposed an adaptive of fixed DTPC) problems in adaptive the approach district the a nodes algorithms have scheme computing

In [12], Niranjan Kumar Ray, Ashok Kumar Turuk have proposed three energy efficient techniques for network environment to reduce energy consumption at protocol level. The first technique minimizes route request message. Second technique optimizes the transmission power at each node and third techniques increases network capacity by topology control mechanism.

Shan Lin et.al in their paper [13] have developed a mechanism where each node builds a model for each of its neighbors, describing the correlation between transmission power and link quality. With this model, feedback transmission power control algorithm dynamically maintain individual link quality over time, basic concepts and applications are dealt with finesse by the authors in [14].

Jasmine Norman in their paper[15] have developed Random Geometric Graphs a very influential and well-studied model of large networks, such as sensor networks, where the network nodes are represented by the vertices of the RGG, and the direct connectivity between nodes is represented by the edges. This assumes homogeneous wireless nodes with uniform transmission ranges. In real life, there exist heterogeneous wireless networks in which devices have dramatically different capabilities. The connectivity of a WSN is

39

related to the positions of nodes, and those positions are heavily affected by the method of sensor deployment. As sensors may be spread in an arbitrary manner, one of the fundamental issues in a wireless sensor network is the coverage problem. study connectivity and coverage in hybrid WSN based on dynamic random geometric graph.

B.Baranidharan in their paper[16] have energy efficiency in wireless sensor network [WSNs] is the highly sorted area for the researchers. Number of protocols has been suggested for energy efficient information gathering for sensor networks. These protocols come under two broad categories called tree based approach and clustering techniques. In these techniques clustering is more suitable for real time applications and has much more scalability factor when compared with its previous counterpart. It presents the importance and factors affecting the clustering. Surveyed the different clustering algorithms with its extensions till date and proposed the clustering technique using Minimum Spanning Tree [MST] and shortest path concept with its strength and limitations.

In the newly formed clusters, the node with the highest energy level is selected as the cluster head and the next higher energy level node is selected as the next CH node. To maintain the stability within the clusters, next CH nodes were selected. Once the cluster head are selected, it generates the TDMA schedule for its cluster members and broadcasts to its cluster members.

In order to reduce further energy wastage due to data transmission between the long distanced Cluster head and sink node, multi-hop data transmission takes place. The data from the nearby cluster heads to the sink node will be directly transmitted to the sink node whereas the data from the distanced cluster head will be transmitted through the shortest multi-hop path.

Shan Lin in their paper [17] have extensive empirical studies presented in this paper confirm that the quality of radio communication between low power sensor devices varies significantly with time and environment. This phenomenon indicates that the previous topology control solutions, which use static transmission power, transmission range, and link quality, might not be effective in the physical world. To address this issue, online transmission power control that adapts to external changes is necessary. This paper presents ATPC, a lightweight algorithm of Adaptive Transmission Power Control for wireless sensor networks. In ATPC, each node builds a model for each of its neighbors, describing the correlation between transmission power and link quality.

CHAPTER 6

PROPOSED WORK

6. 1 Network Structure

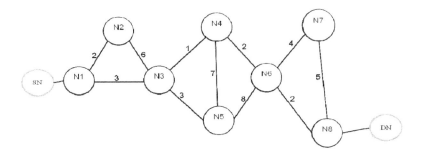

Figure 6.1: Pictorial Representation of Network Structure

The main objective of the project is to develop an adaptive transmission power technique using signed graph approach. The Signed Graph based Adaptive Transmission Power (SGATP) is developed to prolong the lifetime of WSN by reducing the communication mechanism with reduced processing and network power consumption. The basic ideology behind this novel method is to reduce the transmission power of the node automatically so that the communication happens on a one to one basis.

The concept of the adaptive transmission technique is best implemented with Graph Theory. In Graph Theory, the nodes are treated as vertices and the links between them are considered as edges of the graph. Consider the network shown in Figure 14. This Project presents is to detect the shortest path between the neighbor nodes in the given network structure to transmitted the power and improve the network life time of the network using Graph theory. It includes five phases to improve the network performance using adaptive

41

transmission technique. The simplest algorithm is to assign an arbitrarily chosen transmission power level to all sensor nodes, much like it would be done at production time for sensors that do not have power control at all. In the following we assume that the target configuration (i.e., the density of nodes) is known and hence the minimum transmission power providing a fully connected network is known as well. This value is used as fixed transmission power. Additionally larger transmission values are used to show the effect of setting the power level too high.

- Among the node pairs that are not yet connected, choose the one with the smallest distance.
- Set transmission power of all nodes to a value sufficient to connect these two nodes.
- Check connectivity of the resulting network and when the network is connected, the minimum power level is found; otherwise start from 1.

This power value represents the smallest value for a fully connected sensor network with fixed transmission range and it also results in symmetric communication links. This algorithm uses global information and it is not evident how to implement a corresponding local algorithm that achieves the same results. This algorithm minimizes the overall transmission power consumption for the entire network, but it may result in asymmetric communication links, e.g., one node can receive data from a far neighbor which uses a higher transmission power, but can not answer directly due to its smaller transmission power.

The proposed algorithm - SGATP involves five different phases:

- Inter-node distance calculation
- Neighbor nodes Detection
- Shortest Path Calculation
- Adaptive Transmission of Power
- Calculation of Power Consumption of the Network

6.2 Inter-node distance calculation

The sensors are deployed randomly in a WSN. The distance between the sensor nodes need to be calculated to know the neighboring nodes of a particular node. Calculating the distance from the node also helps in finding the amount of power required to reach the next neighbor node. The distance of all other nodes from each node is found by just reading the x and y coordinates of each node in a localized network.Once the coordinates of each node (x, y) are obtained, the inter distance between each node from every other node can be calculated using the two point distance formula given as in equation (1),

$$D = \sqrt{(y_2 - y_1)^2 + (x_2 - x_1)^2} \quad \ldots\ldots\ldots\ldots\ldots\ldots\ldots\ldots\ldots\ldots\ldots\ldots\ldots \quad (1)$$

where 'D' is the distance, (x_1, y_1) and (x_2, y_2) are the coordinates of the nodes.

ALGORITHM 1: Inter Node Distance Calculation

1: **if** *Distance of node i from node i* **then**

2:      *Distance* ⟵   *0*

3: **else** *Distance of node i from node j*

4:      *calculate the distance using the formula*

5: **end if**

The Algorithm 1 explains the steps in calculating the distances from all other nodes from each node.

6.3 Neighboring Node Detection

The inter-node distances help in calculating the number of neighbors to each node. Algorithm 2 gives the flow in which the neighbors are found out. From the internode distance calculation, if the distance is less than the sensing radii of the sensor node then both the nodes are said to be neighboring nodes. Network nodes are represented by the vertices and also direct connectivity between the nodes by the edges. Sensor nodes are maximum flow from one node to the other node to calculate the distance. The Combinatorial Structure are called as network structure. The Number of vertices are connected to the source node in a network is called its neighbor node and the number of edges are its size. Two or more edges of a network joining the same pair of vertices are called multiple edges and corresponding network is known as multipath network shows in table 6.1.   **Table 6.1: Identification of Neighbouring Node.**

Node	Neighboring Node	Edges
N1	N2,N3	2
N2	N3	1
N3	N4,N5	2

43

N4	N5,N6	2
N5	N6	1
N6	N7,N8	2
N7	N8	1
N8	N9	1

ALGORITHM 2: Neighbour Node Detection

1: *Assume a threshold coverage range say 50m for a nodes*

2: **if** *Node i* = *Node j* **then**

3:     **if** *Distance of a node i is less than from node j by 50m*

4:             *Node j is a neighbour of Node i*

5:     **end if**

6: **end if**

6.4 Shortest Path Calculation

The Inter-node distance calculation and the neighborhood discovery form the basis for finding the shortest path that can be taken to communicate between the source and the destination with reduced power requirement thereby prolonging the life time of the network

ALGORITHM 3: Shortest Path Calculation

1: **for all** *nodes in the network*

2: *Calculate the number of neighbours (edges) from that particular node*

3: *From the number of edges calculate the edge with the least weight*

4: *The other end of the edge forms the next neighbour.*

5: *Update a list with the selected neighbours.*

6:     **if** *calculated neighbour of a node is present in the updated list* **then**

7:             *Calculate the next least weight of that neighbour to that node*

8:     **end if**

44

9: **end for**

10. *The number of nodes*

Algorithm 3 explicates the steps involved in finding out the shortest path from the source to the destination.

After finding the shortest path, from the signed and unsigned means of graph representation, the existence of communication link between the edges can be easily determined. For the sample network shown in Figure 6.1, the signed graph representation is shown in Figure 6.2.

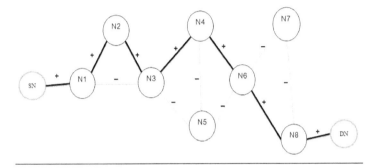

Figure 6.2 Signed representation of the network

On applying the signed graph theory representation of the sample network shown in Figure 1, a '+' in the edges of Figure 6.2 represents a communication link between nodes and a '-' represents no communication link available. Once the signed representation of the network is created using graph theory and the shortest distance with least weight is determined, the algorithm for adaptive transmission between nodes is performed for efficient utilization of power in the network.

6.5 Adaptive Transmission and Calculation of Power Consumption

Finding the shortest distance from the source to the destination helps to find the route the data has to travel without travelling any redundant paths. The objective of adaptive transmission is to find the shortest distance from the node to the next neighbor. The technique uses extra hardware for adjusting the transmitted power and it does so to transmit only to the neighbor with the least distance from it and not to any other node. This avoids unwanted information reaching the sensor nodes and thereby reducing their power consumption by making it forfeit their processing and sensing power. The total power consumed is obtained from the formula given in (2).

In wireless sensor networks, the nodes are read the number of edges from the source node to the neighbour node. First we initialize the transmission power is denoted X. If the node i is less than number of edges then get the distance between the edges to transmitted power in the networks. If the Edges is less than the distance, write down the transmitted power and then calculate the total transmitted power consumed value. Final we calculate the Total power consumed of the whole networks

Power Consumed = Number of nodes * (Sensing Power + Processing Power)........... (2)

ALGORITHM 4: Calculation of Power Consumption

1 : *Assume a value for the transmitting power of the sensor node*

2 : **For** *all node in the updated list*

3 :   **For** *any node i calculate the neighbour node with the least distance*

4 :   *Adjust the transmission power of node i in accordance with the distance.*

5 :   **end for**

6 : **end for**

7 : **For** *the number of nodes in the updated list*

8 :   *Calculate the power consumed by using the formula*

9 : **end for**

10 : **For** *the number of nodes in the network*

11 :   *Calculate the power consumed by using the formula*

12 : **end for**

13 : *Compare the results of power consumed with SGATP with that of power consumed without SGATP*

Using algorithm 4 the transmitted power is made to adapt itself to the distance with least weight calculated with respect to a node.

CHAPTER 7

SOFTWARE CHOSEN

7 SOFTWARE CHOSEN

- C++ Simulator

7.1 Introduction of C++ Simulator

C++ is a complex and powerful programming language. While C++ is not as good as assembly in some areas, it is the most common and powerful language most people use. Most computer software are designed in C++ or any of the other C derivatives, and most operating systems are designed in assembly language. So, if you decide to write programs, C++ is the most powerful and best way to do it. The question that arises is if C++ is worth the trouble with what you want to do. If you are fine with losing very little performance for basic applications, I would recommend C# or other easier languages instead. If you need the speed, high demanding game development for example, you should learn C++. Each language has their own advantages and disadvantages, so the decision is ultimately up to you. C++ (like most OOP languages) is special in that it supports multiple programming paradigms, including object-oriented and procedural. OOP is a paradigm that organizes your application into objects that interact with one another to accomplish a task. With OOP, you can make classes and objects of classes (known as instances of a class) in your program. Later in the basic sub-series, we will have a look at polymorphism, inheritance, and encapsulation. Procedural simply groups a program into operations that are performed. While C++ is one of the most powerful languages around, there are certain disadvantages to it over other languages.

C is a general-purpose high level language that was originally developed by Dennis Ritchie for the Unix operating system. It was first implemented on the Digital Equipment Corporation PDP-11 computer in 1972.

The Unix operating system and virtually all Unix applications are written in the C language. C has now become a widely used professional language for various reasons.

- Easy to learn
- Structured language
- It produces efficient programs.
- It can handle low-level activities.
- It can be compiled on a variety of computers.
- C++ requires that private implementation details of a class be declared in the same declaration in the same declaration as the public interface details. If a change is made to a private definition, then all source code files that depend on the class definition are recompiled.
- Certain changes to the public interface definitions unnecessarily cause recompilation. For eg: adding a public method should not cause dependent objects to be built the interface has not changed in an incompatible manner.
- C++ must explicitly include definitions for any classes that are required to compile.
- Source files should include only those definitions that are necessary in order to compile.
- Many C++ systems do not support pre-compiled headers. Such systems spend a lot of time analzing header definitions code

7.2 Facts about C

C was invented to write an operating system called UNIX.

- C is a successor of B language which was introduced around 1970
- The language was formalized in 1988 by the American National Standard Institue (ANSI).
- By 1973 UNIX OS almost totally written in C.
- Today C is the most widely used System Programming Language.
- Most of the state of the art software have been implemented using C

48

7.3 Usage of C Language

C was initially used for system development work, in particular the programs that make-up the operating system. C was adoped as a system development language because it produces code that runs nearly as fast as code written in assembly language. Some examples of the use of C might be:

- Operating Systems
- Language Compilers
- Assemblers
- Text Editors
- Print Spoolers
- Network Drivers
- Modern Programs
- Data Bases
- Language Interpreters
- Utilities

7.4 C Program File

All the C programs are written into text files with extension ".c" for example *hello.c* into a file.

This states that editing a text file and writing programming instructions inside a program file.

7.5 C Compilers

To write any program in C language then to run that program,compile is needed in that program using a C Compiler which converts your program into a language understandable by a computer. This is called machine language (ie. binary format). So before proceeding, make sure you have C Compiler available at your computer. It comes along with all flavors of Unix and Linux.

However, if you get used to C++, the advantages are well worth it. Here is a list of advantages and disadvantages:

7.6 Advantages

- More User Control
- Manual Memory Management
- Incredible Speed
- Widely Supported

7.7 Disadvantages

- Requires More Work
- Pointers and Memory Management

CHAPTER 8

RESULTS AND DISCUSSION

8.1 Simulation Results

It is assumed that the network setup is static, meaning that the location of the sensor nodes does not change. It is also assumed that the sensor nodes have the same transmitting power. In the simulation of the network the number of the nodes is entered. Based on the number of nodes the topology of the network is determined. The topology of the network for the number of nodes to be 10 is shown in **Figure 8.1**.

Figure 8.1 Network Topology for 10 Nodes

The nodes are represented as vertices and are shown as circles with the node ID inside the circle. The communication links between nodes are the edges and they are gives as directed lines between them. It is assumed that Node 1 is the source and the value of the number of nodes in the network is the destination.

For this topology the inter-node distance between nodes is calculated and the neighbor discovery process leads to the number of neighbors for each and every node. It is assumed that the nodes within the coverage range of 50m of a particular node are considered to be the neighbors of that node. The Adjacency matrix is determined from the neighbor detection method and for **Figure 8.1** it is shown in **Table 8.1**.

Table 8.1. Adjacency Matrix for the 10 Node Network

Node	1	2	3	4	5	6	7	8	9	10
1	0	1	1	1	0	1	0	1	1	1
2	1	0	1	1	1	1	0	1	1	1
3	1	1	0	1	1	1	1	1	1	1
4	1	1	1	0	1	1	1	1	1	1
5	0	1	1	1	0	1	1	1	1	1
6	1	1	1	1	1	0	0	1	1	1
7	0	0	1	1	1	0	0	0	0	1
8	1	1	1	1	1	1	0	0	1	1
9	1	1	1	1	1	1	0	1	0	1
10	1	1	1	1	1	1	1	1	1	0

From the above table, it is interpreted that the entries having a '1' are the nodes that are neighbors of a particular node. For example, for Node 1, Nodes 2, 3, 4, 6, 8, 9 and 10 are neighbors since they fall under the coverage range of Node 1. After determining the neighbors the least distance among the neighbors from a node is calculated and the process proceeds in a similar fashion for the shortest distance between the source and the destination is found out. The signed graph shown in Figure 8.2 clearly indicates the communication links retained ('+' sign in the graph) and the links rejected ('-' sign in the graph).

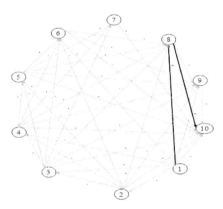

Figure 8.2. Signed representation of the 10 Node network

8.2 Getting the Number and edges of Nodes

Simulated Results are done by using the C++ simulator. **Figure 8.3** we consider the read the number of node in a network.

Figure 8.3: Read the Number of Node

8.3 Calculation of Neighbors Node

Figure 8.4 shows the number of edges from the neighbour node and also calculate the distance between the edges.

```
"G:\M.E PROJECT\Kanna\neighbour1.exe"
Enter the Number of Nodes in the Network        3
The Number of Nodes in the Network        3
Enter the Edges for Node1:2
Enter the Edges for Node2:1
Enter the Edges for Node3:2
CALCULATION OF NEIGHBORS

Enter the Neighbours of Node 1:
2
3
Enter the Neighbours of Node 2:
3
Enter the Neighbours of Node 3:
4
5
The Neighbours of Node 1 are:     2        3
The Neighbours of Node 2 are:     3
The Neighbours of Node 3 are:     4        5

Enter the Distance between Edges :
```

Figure 8.4 : Number of Edges from the Neighbor Node

53

8.4 Calculation of Shortest Path

Figure 8.5 shows the distance between each edges of the neighbour node and then calculate the shortest path in a network.

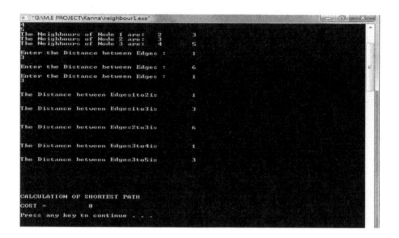

Figure 8.5 : Shortest Path Calculation

8.5 Calculation of Power Consumption of the Network

Assuming the transmission power to be 6mW and sensing power to be 2mW, the power consumption of the network is calculated by executing the algorithm and by substituting the required values in (2). The following simulation results were obtained as given in **Table 8.2.**

Table 8.2. Simulation result of Power Consumed in the Network

No of Nodes	X	Y
5	80	24
10	192	24
13	320	8
14	256	8
16	472	24
20	384	8
22	728	24
25	1808	48
26	1608	24
30	440	8

X - Power Consumed without SGATP in mW
Y - Power Consumed with SGATP in mW

Table 8.2 shows the simulated result of the proposed method where it is inferred that the Power consumption is greatly reduced when the concept of adaptive transmission based on distance is taken into consideration.

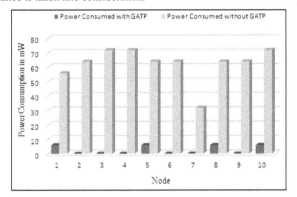

Figure 8.6. Power Consumption of Individual Nodes

From Figure 8.6, it is clearly understood that the power consumption of the individual nodes is more when there is no adaptive transmission in power whereas it is reduced to a greater extent when SGATP is implemented. When the individual nodes' power consumption is reduced it means that the network life time is extended. This is inferred from Figure 8.7.

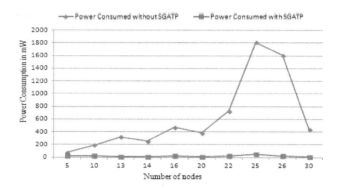

Figure 8.7. Comparison of power consumption with and without SGATP

Figure 8.7 shows the comparison graph between two techniques where it is inferred that the proposed graph theory based adaptive transmission technique reduces the redundant processing of data by nodes which greatly reduces the power consumption of the node. From Figure 8.6 and Figure 8.7 it is clearly seen that using SGATP, the power consumption of individual nodes is greatly reduced thereby enhancing the life time of the network.

CHAPTER 9

CONCLUSION AND FUTURE WORK

Extending the life of the WSN is a challenge and to address this parameter of importance, a Novel algorithm SGATP is developed. Simulation results show a considerable decrease in the Power consumption of individual nodes. Moreover, the results reveal that when the number of nodes in the network increases there is no alarming increase in the power consumption. As there is a substantial reduction in the power consumption of individual nodes the overall network lifetime is greatly enhanced. This is done mainly by altering the transmission power of the node based on the distance of its immediate neighbor. The usefulness of the proposed algorithm can be realized in Intrusion detection.

During Intrusion detection in sensor networks, some genuine nodes need to communicate with the Cluster Head (CH) to inform about the details of malicious nodes and finally the CH validates and informs the other nodes about the intruder. In this scenario, when a node transmits data to a destination node, the data can be sent without being overheard by the neighboring nodes thereby reducing the wastage in power consumption.

SGATP which has been proved to be efficient in improving the life of the network has future scope in the aspect that: The network is assumed to be static where this proposed algorithm can be implemented for a dynamically changing topology where the issue of information transfer in WSN after nodes leave the network due to its exhaustion of energy can be addressed to.

REFERENCES

[1] Sorooshyari. S, Gajic Z, "Autonomous Dynamic Power Control for Wireless Networks: User-centric and Network centric consideration", IEEE Trans. On Wireless Communications. Vol. 7, Issue 3. Pp 1004-1015. March 2008.

[2] Correia L.T.H.A., Macedo D.F., Silva D.A.C., Santos A.L.D., Loureiro A.A.F. and Noguerira J.M.S., "Transmission Power Control in MAC Protocols for Wireless Sensor Networks", Proc. of the 8th ACM/IEEE International Symposium on Modelling, Analysis and Simulation of Wireless and Mobile Systems (MSWiM'05), Montreal, Quebec, Canada, 2005. Pp 282- 289.

[3] Arnab Nandi, Sumit Kundu "On Energy Level Performance of Adaptive Power Based WSN in Presence of Fading" , International Journal of Energy, Information and Communications Vol. 3, Issue 2, May, 2012.

[4] Khemapech I., Miller A. and Duncan I., "A Survey of Transmission Power Control in Wireless Sensor Networks", Proc. of the 8th Annual Postgraduate symposium on the Convergence of Telecommunications, Networking and Broadcasting (PGNet 2007). 2007. Pp. 15-20.

[5] Pantazis N.A., Vergados D.D., Miridakis N.I. and Vergados D.J., "Power control schemes in wireless sensor networks for homecare e-health applications", ACM International Conference Proceeding Series, Athens, Greece, 2008.

[6] Kayhan Erciyes , Orhan Dagdeviren , Deniz Cokuslu , Deniz Ozsoyeller, "Graph Theoretic Clustering Algorithms in Mobile Ad hoc Networks and Wireless Sensor Networks - Survey", Appl. Comput. Math. 6 (2007), no.2, pp.162-180.

[7] Jin Wang, Tinghuai Ma, Qi Liu, Sai Ji, Sungyoung Lee, "A Novel Transmission Power Control Approach for Wireless Sensor Networks", Sensor Letters, 2012

[8] Martin Kubisch, Holger Karl, Adam Wolisz, Lizhi Charlie Zhong, Jan Rabaey, "Distributed Algorithms for Transmission Power Control in Wireless Sensor Networks", proceeding of: IEEE Wireless Communications and Networking, 2003

[9] Christopher Grin, "Graph Theory" Penn State Math 485 Lecture Notes Version 1.1, 2011-2012

[10] Monika Bathla, Nitin Sharma, "A Review Paper on Topology Control in Wireless Sensor Networks" IJECT Vol. 2, Issue 2, June 2011

[11] Suman Banerjee, Archan Misra, "Adapting Transmission Power for Optimal Energy Reliable Multi-hop Wireless Communication", Wireless Optimization Workshop (WiOpt'03), Sophia-Antipolis, France, March 2003.

[12] Niranjan Kumar Ray, Ashok Kumar Turuk, "Energy Efficient Techniques for Wireless Ad Hoc Network",

[13] Shan Lin, Jingbin Zhang, Gang Zhou, Lin Gu, Tian He, and John A. Stankovic,"ATPC: Adaptive Transmission Power Control for Wireless Sensor Networks", SenSys '06 Proceedings of the 4th international conference on Embedded networked sensor systems, Pages 223-236

[14] S.G.Shirinivas, S.Vetrivel, N.M.Elango "Applications of Graph Theory in Computer Science - An Overview", International Journal of Engineering Science and Technology, Vol. 2(9), 2010, 4610-4621

[15] Connectivity and Coverage in Hybrid Wireless Sensor Networks using Dynamic Random Geometric Graph Model, Author : Jasmine Norman, Vellore Institute of Technology, Vellore – 14, International journal on applications of graph theory in wireless ad hoc networks and sensor networks (GRAPH-HOC) Vol.3, No.3, September 2011 .

[16] A New Graph Theory based Routing Protocol for Wireless Sensor Networks, Author : B.Baranidharan, B.Shanthi, SASTRA University, School of Computing, Thanjavur, India, International journal on applications of graph theory in wireless ad hoc networks and sensor networks (GRAPH-HOC) Vol.3, No.4, December 2011.

[17] Bhupendra Gupta , Srikanth K Iyer , D Manjunath , "Topological Properties Of The One Dimensional Exponential Random Geometric Graph", Random Structures & Algorithms , Volume 32 , Issue 2 , 2008, pp: 181-204

[18] Chen Avin , "Random Geometric Graphs: An Algorithmic Perspective" , Ph,D dissertation, University of California , Los Angeles , 2006

[19] Chi-Fu Huang, Yu-Chee Tseng , "The Coverage Problem in a Wireless Sensor Network" , WSNA'03,September 19, 2003, San Diego, California, USA.

[20] J. Diaz D. Mitsche X. Pierez-Gimienez , "On the Connectivity of Dynamic Random Geometric Graphs, Symposium on Discrete Algorithms" , Proceedings of the nineteenth annual ACM-SIAM symposium on Discrete algorithms , 2008, pp 601-610

Publisher: Eliva Press SRL

Email: info@elivapress.com

Eliva Press is an independent publishing house established for the publication and dissemination of academic works all over the world. Company provides high quality and professional service for all of our authors.

Our Services:
Free of charge, open-minded, eco-friendly, innovational.

-All services are free of charge for you as our author (manuscript review, step-by-step book preparation, publication, distribution, and marketing).
-No financial risk. The author is not obliged to pay any hidden fees for publication.
-Editors. Dedicated editors will assist step by step through the projects.
-Money paid to the author for every book sold. Up to 50% royalties guaranteed.
-ISBN (International Standard Book Number). We assign a unique ISBN to every Eliva Press book.
-Digital archive storage. Books will be available online for a long time. We don't need to have a stock of our titles. No unsold copies. Eliva Press uses environment friendly print on demand technology that limits the needs of publishing business. We care about environment and share these principles with our customers.
-Cover design. Cover art is designed by a professional designer.
-Worldwide distribution. We continue expanding our distribution channels to make sure that all readers have access to our books.

www.elivapress.com

www.ingramcontent.com/pod-product-compliance
Lightning Source LLC
LaVergne TN
LVHW052314060326
832902LV00021B/3879